BARS
of
IRON

OVERCOME YOUR SETBACKS AND SHATTER YOUR LIMITS

Adekemi Giwa

authorHOUSE®

AuthorHouse™ UK
1663 Liberty Drive
Bloomington, IN 47403 USA
www.authorhouse.co.uk
Phone: 0800.197.4150

Published by AuthorHouse 02/23/2019

ISBN: 978-1-7283-8268-5 (sc)
ISBN: 978-1-7283-8267-8 (e)

Print information available on the last page.

This book is printed on acid-free paper.

CONTENTS

Acknowledgement

I dedicate this work to those angels in human form, whom God used to support me in my time of vulnerability, and I say THANK YOU.

Margaret "Maggie" Monroe, Clare Young, Isobel McLucas, Robert "Rob" Murray, Patricia "Trish" Robertson, my children's "Scottish mothers", Mrs Anne Marie D'Arcy, Mr McSorley, Mrs Wilson, Mandy Wiseman, Ashley Livingston, Gbemisola & Femi Olusola, Mrs Frasier, Mr Kerr, Mrs Warrington, The Segun Ibigbemis.

Reviews

This is an inspiring and challenging book. Adekemi Giwa skilfully captures some of the key reasons why people are not reaching their potential and addresses these issues head on. There are so many stand out phrases that catch your attention, yet there is real depth to her writing that comes from a place of experience and wisdom. I love that this book has broad advice that will have specific applications for different individuals. I look forward to sharing this book with friends.

For people on an upward, hopeful journey regardless of their starting point.

Clare Young
Family Worker, Whiteinch Transformation

This book is an exploration of a very strong person who openly and bravely shares her experiences and, as a result, her outlook on life. The writing is flowing and accessible, and as you go on a journey with this inspiring woman, you will inevitably and positively explore yourself. This book does not simply provide a fleeting inspiration, but substance and a positive impact that stays with you.

Gary Adam
Glasgow, United Kingdom

Adekemi Giwa has written a powerful treatise in this masterpiece BARS OF IRON. Drawing from a wealth of experience, personal revelation, wisdom as well as trials and tribulation, this work is a road map. It is guaranteed to help its readers locate themselves in the midst of their situations and navigate their way into their God given destiny and future. It is simple, insightful and full of nuggets of wisdom. A very well done job by a woman who has learnt the art of making " LEMONADE OUT OF LEMONS".

Olusegun Akinkugbe
Pastor & John C Maxwell Equip Certified Associate Trainer

Preface: What Are Bars of Iron?

Bars of iron are solid and strong. They are not breakable without force and effort. Bars of iron are formidable and impenetrable. They can be intimidating. Bars of iron gives the impression of prison doors, domineering and posing a great hindrance to access. So also are some of life's issues, which tend to hold one down or prevent one from forging ahead in life with some feeling, as if there's no escape. Such experiences include bereavement, divorce, war, tragedy, abuse, loss of a loved one, loss of a support system, relationship breakdown, systemic breakdown, business ruination, disappointment, and harmful cultural values, beliefs, or lifestyle.

Any of these may spiral into antisocial or mental-health challenges: low self-esteem, alcohol addiction, substance abuse, drug addiction, fear, failure, sorrow, mental-health issues (depression, anxiety, panic attacks, mood swings, and so on). The list of life's troubles and woes are endless.

The good news is these life experiences must not define us in any way. They must never be the reason why we 'stop living'. They must not be allowed to limit us.

Many people can be held down by experience, if not quickly tackled such can become a negative defining point in their lives.

Introduction

I n today's world, we face so many challenges and limitations that life expectancy may be decreasing. Some people are so knocked down by life's issues that they are unaware they can actually pull through. Constraints arise because of the events already highlighted above. All these and many more have become strongholds in the lives of many and have made moving on in life difficult.

The essence of this book is, first and foremost, to let you know you're not alone, and, secondly, to let you know there is a way out—if you have the will! As the saying goes, 'Where there's a will, there's a way.'

This book is filled with phrases and quotations that are meant for the reader to reflect on. The wisdom contained within will aid in your personal determination to find your motivation and recovery.

Breaking
And
Removing
Setbacks & strongholds

of

Impossibilities
Regrets
Or
Negativities

The above issues and many more could be the bars of iron in any human life, making progress an arduous task. It doesn't matter at what point of these human limitations or challenges you've found yourself, whether the issues have gone too deep or are just beginning to surface such. There's a way out, if one so desires it!

So, shatter every limitation to achieving your real potential.

This book is born out of the desire to encourage someone and help them start over, as I received encouragement and help at my lowest point in life.

The first step to self-therapy is the realization that one needs help, as many people are often in denial. Having realized the need for help, the second most important step is self-examination—the simple question: who am I (or who am I supposed to be)?

a. a complete loser
b. an unfortunate victim
c. a deserving idiot
d. a broken human being that deserves a second chance

I identify myself with option D, because I know that everyone deserves a second chance in life! If you're like me and believe you want to have another go at life, then this book is meant for you. The next thing to do is retrace one's steps back to where it all went wrong and get ready to

Heal, forgive, amend, start over, and move ahead.

The many quotes in this book can be cut out and placed in strategic places to serve as encouragement and motivation on this journey to self-actualization (or re-actualization), healing, and discovery.

1. Owner's Manual

When a product developer manufactures a product, he or she has a vision in mind as well as a purpose for the product. It would be foolhardy not to use the product according to the owner's vision—the manual.

Therefore, a manufacturer rolls out instructions for use or setup, which is known as an owner's manual or user's manual, the purpose of which is to guide the user into the world of the manufacturer and his or her thoughts or aspirations for the product—maintenance, use, care, longevity—in order to fulfil the purpose of his or her creation, thus giving the user the benefit of maximum utility.

The judicious use of the owner's manual makes the setting up of the product, or use of such product, easy—not to mention that it saves precious time and the frustration of 'trying to figure it out'.

It will not be wrong to say that the manual, whether the owner's or user's, is an important document for product satisfaction, optimal performance, and longevity of the item in question.

Therefore, your life has a lot of use that you might not have discovered yet. Find your purpose and start living your life to the fullest.

It is safe to say you only get the best out of the product when the owner's manual is followed to the letter. It is sheer arrogance and pure ignorance to jettison the owner's manual and try to operate such products according to one's limited understanding. Several reasons can be attributed to this: laziness, stubbornness, wrong attitude, arrogance, parochial mentality, mediocre attitude, and so on. Wisdom enables one to accept instructions to chart unknown terrain. It is imperative to allow instruction to be one's guide in such quest to accomplish the desired results!

Nobody knows you better than yourself and your creator, so no one can write your life's manual like you and the one who created you. Therefore, let no one—I repeat, no one—define you for you. When you're down, you'll get up. If you're burnt out, you will heal!

So go back to your very own owner's manual, which is your dreams, aspirations, desires, goals, and so on, retrace your steps back to where it all went wrong, and start all over from there. Follow your manual's instructions; don't live in denial. Allow the truth to sink in; accept the fact of the situation and do something about it!

What is your own manual? Could it be that dream as a child, as a teenager, or even as a young adult? Could it be that aspiration or desire you had a long time ago? Does it seem unachievable or as if it belongs to some distant past? Do they seem buried in the sand of time?

If given another chance, would you live your life differently? Do you feel that those dreams or aspirations are far-fetched? Do you feel you are too old, too tired, or too worn out to dream again? Or do you feel there's no help in sight to actualize those dreams?

Bring out your 'memoirs'. Bring out that dream; challenge yourself today. Your manual is the map to your destiny. It is an inroad to your purpose, and your purpose is the real you.

Dare to dream again. Dare go back to where it went off, and pick up from right there, or start all over again.

The first point of help is yourself! If you don't help yourself, how will someone else be motivated to help you? There's an old saying: 'Heaven helps those who help themselves.' It is also true that people care about people who care about themselves. Dare to believe in yourself. Pick up your dream—sell your dream to those who will invest in it.

Need to acquire new skills or polish your talent? Do you lack resources or have limited funds? Search for scholarships, mentorships, or charitable organizations that can help you actualize your dream. Look for information to point you to the right path.

The Holy Scriptures—the Bible—says, 'Study to show yourself approved, a workman that need not be ashamed, rightly dividing the word of truth' (1 Timothy 2:15).

The manual referred to in this case—the Holy Bible—says to study. When you 'know', then you have acquired knowledge. When you have knowledge, you have a solution. When you work out solutions, you get results. When you get results, you get rewards.

Look your inhibition in the face and begin to chart your course of action. Your owner's manual is your personal compass to the ultimate life you are meant to achieve. Determine that you are giving yourself another opportunity, and resolve that it will not slip from you this time. Assume through this book that life is giving you another chance and that it would be foolhardy to let go of such opportunity. Make the most of it.

A reward does not bring shame. It brings glory, accolades, joy, fulfilment, gratification, and so on.

The secret of success lies in instructions, timeliness, and obedience.

NOTES TO SELF

1. Therefore, your life has a lot of use that you might not have discovered yet. Find your purpose and start living your life to the fullest.

2. Wisdom enables one to accept instructions to chart unknown terrain.

3. Nobody knows you better than yourself and your creator, so no one can write your life's manual like you and the one who created you. Therefore, let no one—I repeat, no one—define you for you.

4. When you have knowledge, you have a solution. When you work out solutions, you get results. When you get results, you get rewards.

5. The secret of success lies in instructions, timeliness, and obedience.

2. The Blame Game

In different phases of our lives, the results we have attained may not be desirable—sometimes due to our wrong choices or and sometimes due to wrong choices made on our behalf. The latter is more painful because we are not directly responsible. At this point, it is natural to want to 'resolve to fate'—the feeling of 'perhaps that is how it's destined to be.' The 'it's okay not to do anything about it' attitude quickly degenerates into assigning blame: It is my ancestors' fault/my partner's fault/my country's fault/somebody else's fault that I am in this situation.

It is good to identify faults and their origins. What is not good is to allow others' errors or mistakes to shape how your life will eventually turn out. This is a defeatist attitude—otherwise known as being a 'sore loser'.

Phrases like 'I was not brought up in a privileged environment', 'I am not used to things like this', 'I am disadvantaged', 'I'm too old', and many others must be put aside.

Assuming these excuses are genuine—that our upbringing or background or life experiences were at fault and we are helpless—that was then, and this is *now*! There are a million things you can do about it now. If the privilege of now is not utilized, then the circumstantial injustice now becomes one's fault, and we become guilty of helping others spoil our lives!

There is a saying where I came from: 'You are the architect of your misfortune.' Though you were a victim of circumstances, by not doing something about it, you've taken ownership of circumstantial misfortune!

Rise up! It's time to make lemonade out of the lemon life tossed you. Stop playing the blame game. If your parents didn't do much for you, if your upbringing deprived you, then do something about it.

Unfortunately, some people are so delusional with this blame game that they pass up many chances for redemption. They lose many opportunities and privileges to get it right.

The first step in this journey is a change of attitude. Quit blaming others or your circumstances for your current situation. Instead, shout at the top of your lungs, 'It is enough! I am not a loser! I quit my defeatist attitude. I am ready to take on life headlong!'

It is often said, 'If life throws lemons at you, make lemonade'—that is, beat life at its own game and be the champion.

So go back to the drawing board. Identify where and how it went wrong, and let's start this incredible journey of fixing our lives and getting our groove back.

You *can* rewrite your destiny.

> *You should not be afraid of failure. The bottom line is, when you make mistakes, learn as quickly as possible.*
> —Mark Zuckerberg, during his visit to Nigeria in 2016

NOTES TO SELF

1. It is good to identify faults and their origins. What is not good is to allow others' errors or mistakes to shape how your life will eventually turn out.
2. Rise up! It's time to make lemonade out of the lemon life tossed you.
3. Though you were a victim of circumstances, by not doing something about it, you've taken ownership of circumstantial misfortune!
4. beat life at its own game and be the champion.
5. So, go back to the drawing board. Identify where and how it went wrong, and let's start this incredible journey of fixing our lives and getting our groove back.
6. You can re-write your destiny.

3. Introspection (Soul Search)

There's a set way and style you used to do things, but it has not brought the desired results, or it has brought little or no gratification. The time has come to jettison stereotypes. Have a deep soul search and think outside the box.

In this situation, self-truth is necessary. There is this saying in my dialect: 'If others are misleading or deceiving you, don't mislead or deceive yourself!'

Face your truth—the real you—and work out how you can make a not-so-good situation better, or a better situation best. There's always room for improvement.

With soul-searching comes the question: 'How did I get here? How did it get so bad? What was I supposed to have done that I didn't do?' All these questions will lead to a sincere answer. This answer is the foundation for a new beginning!

This is called introspection!

Take yourself out of your familiar territory. Take yourself out of your comfort zone. Expound on past knowledge, lessons, experiences, and so on. Earmark where things went wrong and see what lessons you can extract.

Leave behind the 'This is how we used to do it' syndrome. If it's not working, go for 'How can we do it better?'

Don't let stubbornness or fear get in the way. Sometimes, fear does not allow someone to explore new frontiers. This is given all sorts of names: risk, carefulness.

Do understand a fact today, that 'life itself is a risk'; moving from one place to another is a risk; accidents happen every waking day; nobody plans for an accident; that's why it is called an 'accident' anyways.

Do not allow past hurt to restrain you from moving forward. *Tell yourself, 'The past belongs to what hurt me, but the future belongs to me and me alone.'*

Step outside your comfort zone, do things differently, don't be afraid to take 'calculated risks', think outside the box, be strategic, plan, and work around every limiting factor.

Never be afraid to try something new, stretch your ideas, tear it apart, discuss it with people who can set you in the right direction, if need be. Stay away from negative people who *do not see anything good in anything!*

Introspection is very important. Nobody can assess your situation better than you can – without bias, condemnation, or prejudice.

When we introspect, we have truly begun a journey into deliverance, recovery, and restoration. Everything we discover under this process will serve as the components for our recovery. We will need to identify the people, situations, and circumstances of life that have become the 'cogs in the wheel of our progress or success'.

We will also need to undergo a (probably painful) process called 'separation'. We will need to 'separate the chaff from the wheat', to consciously remove oneself from toxic relationships, acquaintanceship, and environment. This exercise is necessary because we need to disgorge and bring out all the dirt and embark on a thorough cleansing of the spirit, mind, and soul.

Each day, we are faced with situations in which we must make choices or take certain decisions. These choices might be because of helplessness, immaturity, limited resources, or other circumstances. It is a fact that life occurs in stages, and at each stage, we attain a certain measure of maturity. However, introspection helps to identify wrong choices we have made in the past and how to fix them. We look back at our choices, or the effect of such on our lives as we grow up or mature in life, and we desire to amend some of these choices.

Part of the soul search is honestly identifying one's strengths and facing our truth. Some people are meant to be captains of fifties, some captains of hundred, some captains of thousands, while some captains of legions. Know what you are made up for. For example, British Mo Farah is a champion of the marathon and a gold medallist. With the same capacity he has right now, can he compete with Usain Bolt in the sprint? Can Usain run a marathon and win against Mo? Neither answer means each man is not the best in his field. It simply means each man is cut out for different things and can be the best only in his area of core competence.

Simply put, don't run another man's race. Knowing what you're cut out for (your limit) will help to find a lot of joy and contentment in life.

This is what the soul search does: it helps to find or understand your own truth, to know your capabilities, and to be the master in that field.

When you sincerely identify your threshold, then going all the way for it should be your ultimate desire, without looking back.

NOTES TO SELF

1. The time has come to jettison stereotypes.
2. 'If others are misleading or deceiving you, don't mislead or deceive yourself!'
3. Face your truth—the real you—and work out how you can make a not-so-good situation better, or a better situation best. There's always room for improvement.
4. *Tell yourself, 'The past belongs to what hurt me, but the future belongs to me and me alone.'*
5. Never be afraid to try something new, stretch your ideas, tear it apart, discuss it with people who can set you in the right direction.

4. Mediocrity

Lack of drive and motivation (or no motivation), settling for second best, leaving things as it is, average, mundane, outdated norms, fear of challenges associated with success, lack of self-confidence, not striving hard enough to bring out the best in oneself, low self-esteem, complacency, refusing to leave one's comfort zone, lack of sensitivity and sensibility, shoddy way of doing things, "I can't be bothered" attitude, absence of desire or drive for excellence—all these and many more are synonymous with mediocrity.

By being mediocre or surrounding yourself with mediocrity, you are short-changing yourself. It is said that the human brain can do so much but we utilize only a fraction of it every day. Therefore, make good of this naturally-endowed part of our human anatomy, set worthy goals, develop strategies to achieve these goals and stand out, and turn the ordinary into the extraordinary.

To achieve one's desired position in life, you must first *be comfortable in your own skin*. While it is good to have role models, mentors, coaches, and so on, it's imperative to be confident in oneself first and foremost. Realize (with humility) that out of more than 7 billion people on planet earth, there are no two of you! Not even your twin! You're your own unique brand. A glimpse of this is in the Holy Scriptures, where we are made to understand the intricacies and uniqueness of our creation and how we were fearfully (reverently, carefully, delicately) and wonderfully made (Psalms 139:14). Also, it is categorically stated in my own human owner's manual (the Bible) that I am a peculiar people (1 Peter 2:9).

Being comfortable in your skin is accepting yourself for who you are, acknowledging your weaknesses and your strengths, scoring yourself on your strengths and, striving to work on your weaknesses. If you don't believe in yourself, why should someone else believe in you?

The second rule is *Map out your dreams, desires, and goals, and work out how to accomplish them.* In this journey, the heart (intuition/faith) is a constant companion and guide, because there will be decisions you must take and options you must consider. The fact that a route worked for A does not necessarily mean it will be same for B. It's important to remember always that no two destinies are identical. You are your own unique personality. When you settle this thought at the beginning of your new journey, *there won't arise any basis for comparison. Instead, there will be peace, gratitude, and contentment!*

Always bear in mind what works for you and pursue it relentlessly. This is called strategy!

The third rule is *You might not achieve success at the very first attempt.* Neither take no for an answer nor rest on your oars until you achieve your desire!

China is a good example. When I was in my preteens, in the eighties, nobody in my country wanted to acquire anything made in China because they were considered 'inferior products', but today, China, through hard work and dedication, has become a world superpower, playing a role in the economy of every other nation.

Determine that excellence will be your watchword. To do things excellently is to save yourself stress and time. I've found that things done shoddily cost more and waste a whole lot of time.

The fourth rule is *Everybody identifies with excellence.* Nobody identifies with failure. Nothing done shoddily is applauded. Mediocrity does not attract success!

So, we can safely conclude that it is more expensive to live in mediocrity or be a mediocre. Being mediocre is doing a great disservice or injustice to oneself. Why settle for second best when you can have the very best? Mediocrity cannot thrive in the face of competition. Mediocrity is a thief of time. *Don't be robbed.*

My life principle has always been 'Do it right and do it best the very first time', because you might not have another opportunity to prove your mettle. Make up your mind, and make it a principle always to do it right, and do it excellently, the very first time.

Let excellence drive whatever you choose to do in

life. I always feel anyone who offers a mediocre idea or service is a cheat—a cheat to himself, depriving oneself of doing something in a better way, and a cheat to one's end users, because they have not received value for their expectation.

Dream big, think big, desire big!

> *Excellence is the solution to mediocrity.*
> —Pastor Femi Paul (thegraceassembly.org)

> *Be a yardstick of quality. Some people aren't used to an environment where excellence is expected.*
> —Steve Jobs (1955–2011)

NOTES TO SELF

1. To achieve one's desired position in life, you must first be comfortable in your own skin.
2. By being mediocre or surrounding yourself with mediocrity, you are short-changing yourself.
3. The fact that a route worked for A does not necessarily mean it will be same for B.
4. You might not achieve success at the very first attempt.
5. Everybody identifies with excellence. Nobody identifies with failure.
6. Dream big, think big, desire big!

5. Self-SWOT Analysis

In my over a decade experience as a risk manager, I found a theory very useful for me. It is also applicable to personal use. This was a tool that all credit risk officers had to use in their analysis of credit appraisals to determine the viability of such risk when assessing or analysing bank loans. This is known as SWOT analysis.

Strength
Weakness
Opportunity
Threat

SWOT measures the *strength* of the business/credit proposal, the *weakness* identified in this field, *opportunities* that are inherent investing in such business, and, of course, awareness of the *threats* that gnaw at such opportunity. In this instance, the threat is not perceived as a thing of fear or a reason to walk away from such business proposal; rather, safeguards are set up to mitigate such threats.

Likewise, in our personal lives, there is a need to conduct self-SWOT analysis, highlighting one's area of strength on a scale of 1–10, likewise identifying weaknesses, opportunities (in one's immediate as well as remote environment), opportunities, and threats, all on a scale of 1–10.

If job loss or career dissatisfaction is your issue, when testing your 'strength analysis', it is imperative to note that not all people are cut out for white-collar (or desk) jobs. So, one must ask the following questions:

- What is my area of competence?
- What am I good at?
- Am I indeed cut out for an office job?
- What is my skill set?
- What other skill sets do I need to acquire?
- What gives me joy?
- Where do I feel most accomplished or derive maximum satisfaction?

If it's a hobby that gives you the highest score of satisfaction or freedom to do what you want to do, it's time to turn that hobby into a dream job or a means of livelihood.

If you are having relationship issues, you still need self-appraisal. Ask yourself the following questions:

- What is my relationship management like?
- Am I a people person, or do my social interaction skills need sharpening?

- Do I lack the perseverance I need to hold a relationship, or is my tolerance level low?
- Do I have a bad attitude?
- Am I always attracted to the wrong people?
- Do I have habits that put people off?
- Am I a boring person?

It's imperative to note that in analysing your strength, you must draw a limit. This prevents you from going overboard or being overly ambitious. Also, it's important not to underplay things to ensure optimal achievement. Being underperforming or overly ambitious can lead to frustration, anger, dejection and so on, which could degenerate into negative feelings.

However, identifying and settling limits helps one to achieve optimal results; this gives a real sense of accomplishment and, ultimately, contentment.

Truly, contentment is the real accomplishment! Anyone who has achieved contentment (i.e., no bitterness at underperforming or frustration due to excessive ambition) is already a success story.

Success is not defined by having millions of dollars in our bank account. True success is achieving optimally within your limit. Only this gives you a true sense of self-worth and well-being.

NOTES TO SELF

1. In our personal lives, there is a need to conduct self-SWOT analysis.
2. What other skill sets do I need to acquire?
3. it's time to turn that hobby into a dream job or a means of livelihood.
4. What is my relationship management like? Am I a people person, or do my social interaction skills need sharpening?
5. Success is not defined by having millions of dollars in our bank account. True success is achieving optimally within your limit. Only this gives you a true sense of self-worth and well-being.

6. No Pity Party

Never, ever indulge in self-pity. It is a breeding ground for many depravities: helplessness, depression, hatred, unforgiveness, bitterness, pessimism, and so on. The list is endless. Before you know it, you have become a stranger to yourself.

Once these vices find a home, they reproduce geometrically and gain a stronghold on the individual. Instead of focusing on goals, one become distracted from one's well-laid-out purpose and begins to digress, regress, and eventually becoming stagnant, then unproductive and unhappy. The power of creativity is gradually taken from such a fellow. Then a sense of despair or feeling of uselessness creeps in and begins to have a field day. Nothing makes one's sense of self-worth disappear quicker than this.

Pity parties do not allow the 'indulger' to see the next step or the next point of action. Instead of transforming one's hurt to strength, the one who engages in a pity party adopts a 'victim mentality', ensuring a never-ending blame game, in which the blame for one's life is placed on others. Even if it's true that other parties are responsible for one's predicament, one owes oneself the duty of not allowing 'them' to limit one's goal or divert one's focus.

In assessing one's situation, if it is established that the problem or unwanted situation has been induced by a third party, one should rise from the ashes of such degradation, like the Phoenix.

Recognize that life is a race. 'It's not over until it is over', no matter one's age. As long as there's life, there should be hope! When you fall, you can rise again and continue. Life is not a hundred-meter dash. If one way does not work out, another way is worth trying.

So, get up! Dust yourself and tell yourself, 'I can do it. I will do it.'

We learnt in History class that America's sixteenth president, Abraham 'Abe' Lincoln, after many failures, eventually became a president whose legacy remains with us even today. It is said that he once suffered a nervous breakdown, yet he did not wallow in self-pity.

There's a very apt saying: 'Winners don't quit, and quitters don't win.'

Which are you? The choice is yours!

In my life's journey, I've met many people who have suffered tragedies of every kind. I've seen some of these people get up, dust themselves off, and continue their life's races. Today, it's as if they never suffered such setbacks. Likewise, I've encountered people who suffered setbacks and indulged in pity parties, making themselves victims. Unfortunately, they have become victims of their own excuses, living in abject poverty or with unfulfilled dreams!

Even when it's justified, do not allow situation, events, institutions, or people to bring you to the pity party.

Self-pity does no one any good. Just make the best of any situation in which you find yourself and fashion your way out of any unpleasant situation. Muster up your courage and give yourself every encouragement you can gather.

> *Not everyone will be born with a silver spoon, but everyone can feed with a silver spoon: it's a choice.*

NOTES TO SELF

1. Never, ever indulge in self-pity. It is a breeding ground for many depravities
2. Once these vices find a home, they reproduce geometrically and gain a stronghold on the individual. Instead of focusing on goals, one become distracted from one's well-laid-out purpose.
3. Pity parties do not allow the 'indulger' to see the next step or the next point of action.
4. Recognize that life is a race. 'It's not over until it is over'.
5. So, get up! Dust yourself and tell yourself, 'I can do it. I will do it.'

7. Change Your Circle of Influence

What is my circle of influence? In the literary sense, any person, idea, place, or community you have stayed in over a period that has affected your outlook, principles, or personality is your circle of influence. Any place you've been in over time that has not encouraged your progress or whose influence is rubbing off negatively on your ideals is a negative circle of influence.

There is a saying: 'Great minds think alike', so your thought and principles should not be different from your environment. If this place does not evoke the right atmosphere for your creativity or industry, if you don't always get the 'right vibes' or are always confronted with negativity, unfair treatment, or harsh criticism, it may be time to re-evaluate things and give yourself some space.

Such an unhealthy atmosphere breeds unhappiness and frustration and eventually culminates into mediocrity, compromise, dejection, and anxiety. An environment where your good is misunderstood or unappreciated, where you constantly must prove yourself or fight for your self-respect, adversely rubs off on your confidence.

Despite knowing 'who you are' or the potential you carry, an unhealthy environment cannot translate to your 'success story'.

There is this saying in Africa: 'If a leaf gets stuck to a bar of soap for too long, it tends to become soapy.' This is because the soap nature has so much rubbed off on the leaf. If your circle of influence does not bring out the best in you, or recognize the best in you, it is time to change your location before you lose your identity.

This does not necessarily mean moving from one country to another. Instead, you must relocate from your current toxic or de-motivating environment.

If you truly introspect, you might discover that you've begun to lose your identity. This means you are becoming far removed from your own realities. Examples include

- things you were good at before but can't remember how to do anymore
- things you used to enjoy but derive no pleasure from because of the influence of your environment
- standards you once had that you have compromised so badly, you can barely remember what you used to stand for, until you begin to feel, 'This is not me'

It's time to take a break and critically appraise your situation. If your environment is not positively impacting you—and you are not positively impacting it—you must move on, no matter how difficult it may be. Don't become comfortable with mediocrity. Leave your comfort zone, find your purpose, and pursue it.

Ordinarily, life imposes limits, situations impose limits, even people impose limits. Some of these limits might be legitimate, while others are outright preposterous. Legitimate limits are in place for our own good—such as the condition of our health or our belief system (e.g., law of karma, reap what you sow, and so on). Likewise, some limits are not only illegitimate but ridiculous (e.g., you can't do a particular job because of your sex). It is very important to draw the line and define these limits to determine whether they are legitimate.

While I was growing up in the early seventies, I remember that it was something of a 'taboo' for a boy to be found in the kitchen cooking. He got chased out of the kitchen and scolded severely by the elders, especially the male elders. With the benefit of hindsight, it now seems hilarious that such boys were branded as 'lazy' or doing a 'lady's job'.

It was preposterous. If a girl dared fight with boys, she was thought to be lacking in manners. So, how could a girl that dared not fight with boys dream of becoming a professional wrestler? Thank God for brave men like British celebrity chefs Gordon Ramsey and Jamie Oliver. I'm sure I'm not speaking alone when

I say they've inspired us to be more creative in our culinary skills. They did not deprive the world of their talents and went on to be groundbreakers, inspiring thousands of men to emulate their amazing skills.

We can also not forget pacesetters like the late Mary Lillian Ellison (a.k.a., The Fabulous Moolah), who changed the face of women's professional wrestling forever. Or the late Harriet Quimbly, who paved way for thousands of licensed female pilots. It is a personal choice either to accept these limitations or ride right through them and impact the world with your uncommon skills.

People place limits on others out of their own fear; their own fear of failure acts as a discouragement for others. It is also worth noting that some people place imagined limits on their abilities because they are simply afraid of what they might achieve or the phenomenon they might become!

Some place limits out of envy. They want to be the only 'celebrity' in that environment. So, they'd go to any lengths to crush others' aspirations.

Follow your gut feelings. That thought or idea could be the next big thing.

Your circle of influence has got to change!

NOTES TO SELF

1. Any place you've been in over time that has not encouraged your progress or whose influence is rubbing off negatively on your ideals is a negative circle of influence.
2. There is a saying: 'Great minds think alike', so your thought and principles should not be different from your environment.
3. An environment where your good is misunderstood or unappreciated, where you constantly must prove yourself or fight for your self-respect, adversely rubs off on your confidence.
4. If your circle of influence does not bring out the best in you, or recognize the best in you, it is time to change your location before you lose your identity.
5. Leave your comfort zone, find your purpose, and pursue it.
6. Follow your gut feelings. That thought or idea could be the next big thing.
7. It is a personal choice either to accept these limitations or ride right through them and impact the world with your uncommon skills.

8. Say No to No

Today, millions of people suffer from mental health issues due to fear of the unknown, anxieties about the future, or inability to confront life's challenges.

Valuable lives have been lost because of enduring pain or situations one should not have to endure in the first place; we must recognize that there is a fine line between endurance and outright abuse. Many suffer from low self-esteem, putting on an act of bravado, a façade to pull through each day so they feel 'accepted'.

You must take stock of the unhealthy pressure to meet up to certain people's standards, the pressure to constantly prove yourself. Often there is pressure to be someone you were not created to be. People may encourage you to 'think like Paul', 'dress like David', or 'walk like Sue'. You become lost within yourself and suffer a crisis of identity in the name of conformity.

Is there healthy pressure? Healthy pressure is that gentle (and sometimes not so gentle) push to encourage us to be better people or be better at whatever we do in life, that push to encourage us to accomplish our dreams and aspirations. Unhealthy push does not encourage. In fact, it creates burdens in a bid to fulfil 'unrealistic' goals. It elicits feelings of suffocation and creates a toxic situation which is highly counterproductive. It engenders low self-esteem.

Determine to choose the course your life should run, how you can find happiness in uncomplicated and straightforward things.

My life is my personal gift from my creator. Not even my twin has a right to 'my life'. It is exclusively mine. Therefore, I am responsible to no one how I live this 'life' except the One who gave it to me.

Unhealthy endurance is not a virtue! A life of perpetual sorrow, sadness, or distress is not a virtue.

Tell yourself, 'I am coming out.' Say no to no!

Extricate yourself from the limitation others' views or opinions have placed on you. Absolve yourself totally from the negativity of imposed views or beliefs. Some people are just bitter by nature and are successful in spreading bitterness. One should not be caught up with such people. Distance yourself from acquaintances who are not impacting your life or self-esteem positively. Learn to hold on to your good self, values, and beliefs, even the unpopular ones. Others around you might not encourage your 'positive' views. This should not matter to you. As the old saying goes, 'One with God is a majority', so never be swayed by negative people, no matter their percentage. Remember, your aspirations are quite different from theirs.

Don't partner with people that do not understand the plan!
—Pastor Femi Paul (thegraceassembly.org)

I've found myself amid people who celebrated the mediocre, feebleminded, and visionless. Not only did they snigger at good suggestions and excellent contributions, but they outright rejected any such positive things simply because they did not possess them. These are vision killers, de-motivators, and you have no business hanging around with them. They pay lip service to what is excellent, but when it's time for execution, they are thousands of miles away.

Learn to say no to such people. Learn to motivate yourself in such an environment. Learn to stay true and focused to your vision. Never let such a crowd break your resolve to excel.

When I was very young. I always wanted the best things of life, but I was not fortunate to grow up in an environment that encouraged such. Instead, I endured the taunts and jibes of others. This nearly derailed me, but as I got older, providence guided my path to mentors with whom I share same outlook towards life and my God-given vision. Although it took me another decade or two to align myself, I resolved to pursue excellence and dared to be positively and outstandingly different.

Say no to dream/vision manipulators. Learn to move away from de-motivation. Due to constraints, it may not be easy to move physically. However, guard your vision jealously and don't lose yourself. Say no to anything that wants you to compromise your focus, values, or virtues. Learn to say no to anything at all that will not yield back to you at least 75 per cent return on your expectations, dreams, and aspirations.

Say no to situation, occasion, or environments that do not cater to your spiritual, physical, emotional, or psychological well-being. Say no to anything that reminds you of past failures and anchors you to your past. Learn to say no to mental or emotional abuse. Say no to anything that wants to steal your peace, aspirations, time, or resolve.

Whatever that is not lovely, that does not promote excellence or your inner wellbeing, must end now! So, say no to anything that promotes negativity your life, anything whatsoever that enables resentment. It is toxic.

A lot of 'negative' or 'toxic' people did not start out that way; nor were they created to be so. Life's issues and pressures made them as such, and without realizing it, these people gradually slipped into this negative mode as a defensive mechanism, subconsciously accepting defeat or failure.

Say no to the crowd that believes age should be a barrier to accomplishments. ('You're too old to do this', 'You're too young to do that', 'You're talking beyond your years', 'What do you know?' 'What would the world say?' The list is endless.)

Nothing should be a barrier to reinventing yourself, not even the silly notion of age.

NOTES TO SELF

1. **Valuable lives have been lost because of enduring pain or situations one should not have to endure in the first place.**
2. **Determine to choose the course your life should run, how you can find happiness in uncomplicated and straightforward things.**
3. **Some people are just bitter by nature and are successful in spreading bitterness. One should not be caught up with such people.**
4. **Learn to stay true and focused to your vision. Never let such a crowd break your resolve to excel.**
5. **Nothing should be a barrier to reinventing yourself, not even the silly notion of age.**

9. There's Ability in Inability (Note to Self)

A bility in inability seems contradictory! That is the idea. There are possibilities in impossibilities. There is hope in what seems hopeless.

If asked to define inability, we tend to define it as an impediment, or something that makes us helpless. For some people, their inability to get that dream job resulted from a lack of formal qualification. Inability for some is not knowing their purpose in life. For some, it stems from grief, some ill-health, some lack of motivation or self-confidence, some self-pity, and others not letting go of the past or unforgiveness. For these people, it is impossible to forge ahead.

Yet, even in that seemingly hopeless situation, there's greatness in you!

But you must dare to dream again, dare to hope again, give yourself a chance to believe again.

Remember, aspects of your personality that you believe are holding you back are just what somebody else is praying for.

There's this saying in my mother tongue: 'If you are sorry you have no shoes, someone else is crying because they have no feet.'

Another one: 'In the colony of the blind, the one-eyed man is king.'

As funny as these sayings might sound, the moral is that we should be grateful and hopeful no matter our situation.

By ourselves, we can carve out possibility out of our impossible situation. About twenty years ago, who would have said that America would one day be ruled by a black man? I'm sure this would have sounded preposterous! Impossible! Absurd! Yet, thanks to Mr. Barack Obama, who dared to dream the impossible, this became a reality!

We've all heard the stories of great achievers, such as Bill Gates, Mark Zuckerberg, Sir Richard Branson, and Malala Yousafzai, to mention but a few. They defied the odds to accomplish greatness.

The three gentlemen mentioned above had a common denominator. They were said to have dropped out of school at some point. Across the world, millions drop out of school for one reason or another. How many of these were fortunate to achieve greatness like these men? As many as dared to dream of such fortune, I believe. The fact that Mr. Gates dropped out of school did not mean his story ended there. Instead, it was the beginning of a new journey, the pursuit of greatness!

Dropping out of school may be a form of disability in a very real sense, because education truly is the gateway out of impoverishment. These men did not just drop out of school and fold their hands. Instead, they pursued their dreams (greatness), whereas others who dropped out (quite possibly due to helplessness) but allowed their story to end there.

So what if you don't have formal training or formal qualification? There's possibility in impossibility. So what if you don't have the required resources to start big? There's ability in inability. So what if you've been so battered by life that you feel suffocated? There's ability in inability.

These constraints and many more should not be the end of the matter. Pursue what you believe in, protect your ideas (legally), and then seek people or organizations that can help you turn your dreams into reality.

As you advance in pursuit of your dreams, note every lesson learnt and continue to apply effort until you can educate yourself further. If you still cannot afford formal education, seek informal education. Thank God for technology!

The Internet contains millions of links to enlighten your mind further. In a bid to do this, ensure you access the right stuff. Likewise, make use of your local library. Borrow books on ideas you are interested in and educate yourself. Join book clubs. There is a book in the *Dummies* series on practically every subject. Enlighten yourself, invest in yourself, and build up your reservoir of knowledge.

Wherever am privileged to hold talks, I often say

to people, 'Nobody can take what you know from you.' Knowledge, as they say, is power.

Encourage yourself and pick up from where you stopped. It is not the end. See where you stopped as a bend in the road and continue to pursue your dreams. The fact that that there is an 'impossible' aspect of your life does not necessarily mean an end in other aspects. You are stronger than you think.

British mogul Sir Richard Branson was dyslexic and dropped out of school at 16. The amazing thing was that, in spite of his condition, he went on to start his own business. His 'disability' in no way hindered his dreams or his pursuit of greatness.

From the moment Robert encouraged me to compile my life lessons into a book until the time I contacted my publisher took over two years. Over two years of struggle with ill health, my two son's health challenges, threat of homelessness, and financial hardships, to mention just a few. In spite of all these, I continued writing. There were days, even weeks, when I could not articulate my thoughts to continue with my manuscripts. There were days of interruption because we needed to go into hospital for admissions or for unending tests. I knew I had to get my experience or lessons learnt out there. Perhaps this will give a person or two hope in their personal struggles.

There is hope in that situation you think is hopeless, 'enable' your 'unable' and give expression to your strength.

The world heard about the bravery of a young girl

named Malala Yousafzai, who was an activist for female education in Pakistan and was shot at by the Taliban. She was brought to the United Kingdom between life and death for treatment. After her recuperation, she continued her campaign for her cherished cause.

As a mother, I could relate to the millions of mothers who would have tried to discourage their daughters, saying, 'Enough is enough', but she was not deterred by the attack. Instead, she was quoted as saying, 'I don't want to be known as "a girl shot at by the Taliban" but as "the girl who fought for education".' It was evident that she chose the path to create abilities for others out of her own disabilities.

NOTES TO SELF

1. There are possibilities in impossibilities.
2. Nothing should be a barrier to reinventing yourself, not even the silly notion of age.
3. Remember, aspects of your personality that you believe are holding you back are just what somebody else is praying for.
4. There's this saying in my mother tongue: 'If you are sorry you have no shoes, someone else is crying because they have no feet.'
5. If you still cannot afford formal education, seek informal education. Thank God for technology!

10. Transformation Process

To be transformed is to evolve from one form to another, to change from the status quo. We all have the ability to evolve. Evolution can be either positive or negative. The choice is personal!

To be successful in whatever one does, or in achieving one's life goals, a transformation must occur—of mindset, ideas, principles, beliefs, faith, culture, and so on. Transformation of mindset is very germane, as a person with a mediocre or parochial mentality will have little chance for success in this technologically-driven age.

Everything starts from the mind—ideas, belief, norms, decisions, culture, and so on. It's only natural that the decision to excel also must start from the mind. One must convince oneself of the need for change. The major factor for transformation is to change one's mindset, attitude, lifestyle, habits, and so on. It is often said, 'You can't do things the same way and expect different results.'

As we know, transformation is another word for

change. Hence, refusing change is tantamount to short-changing oneself. Therefore, embrace change all the way!

Transformation is an exciting process that contains enduring lessons along the way.

As the saying goes 'Variety is the spice of life', so, jumping on the bandwagon of the change process, one will meet up with self-denial, sacrifice, self-discovery, and excitement. Gains from transformation are innovations, ideas, information, and so on.

To achieve distinction, one must be transformed in thought, adopting beliefs inimical to acceptable standards and embracing new ideas, new discoveries, new knowledge. The Holy Scriptures attest to this, in the book of Romans 12:2, 'And be not conformed to this world, but be ye transformed by the renewing of your mind' (AKJV).

Not conforming to the norm is acceptable where the norm is mediocrity, complacency, compromise, or risk-averseness.

To attain new heights, one must challenge oneself to rise above board, to embrace a mindset of excellence and possibilities, distinction and grace.

Change, or the desire for change, enables one to see new ideas—or even old ones from a new perspective. This prevents rigidity that often accompanies frustration and failure.

It will therefore not be an error to say that anyone who does not become transformed or allow themselves the privilege of transformation is 'so yesterday'.

To succeed, get transformed through continuous rebuilding, re-branding, personal reappraisal, research, reflections, discussions, mentoring, studying—the list is endless.

Transformation is also creating something out of nothing. Ideas (visions) touched with action and resulting in the envisioned reality have encountered the power of transformation! Transformation births creativity, prohibits rigidity, and amounts to high productivity. When we allow ourselves to be enrolled in the school of transformation, we will be free from the prison of rigidity, of our outdated mentality.

Transformation is akin to getting a 'total makeover'. As the word implies, a makeover is a total overhaul or refurbishment of an old item to improve upon it. The first noticeable part of anything that undergoes a makeover is one's appearance. As one changes, one's appearance becomes more appealing and exciting. This also holds true in the case of transforming oneself or one's ideas. Transformation opens a new door to advanced ways of life, associations, interactions, and so on, it makes life a lot more fun, which in turn opens the doors of great possibility.

Acquiring new knowledge is vital for a true transformation. After all, if it's done the old way, nothing has changed!

Time is also an important factor in a true transformation process. Give yourself time to put all the knowledge into use. It's also important to put time to optimal use by setting a target on the turnaround time so that time is properly managed.

For the transformation process to be successful, it is beneficial to be a fast leaner; this allows one to recoup wasted time and resources.

Don't procrastinate. Let loose. Adopt the transformation process. Don't allow the old mindset, which was obviously not working, bind you. Be determined to change for the better. Break the barriers. Discover new frontiers. Set new targets. Accomplish new goals.

Don't conform. You can't put new wine in old wineskin. Transformation comes from the renewing of the mind, so one needs to regenerate one's belief system all the time. There's a need to update the mind. Trends change at jet speed. Knowledge needs updating continuously. It is easy to be left behind or become out of touch in a world where technology brings global knowledge to your doorstep.

There's a constant need to do away with outdated belief systems. Unfortunately, due to long-term trauma or suffering, it is very easy to get stuck in the 'victim mentality'. Therefore, one needs to purge the mind of suffering. Whatever negative experience life thrusts at you, you need to shake it off before it gets hold of you, making it more difficult to dislodge its grip. Whatever situation you've been in for so long tends to influence your perspective on things, both generally and specifically. You must remove yourself from such hold, consciously uncouple yourself from such grip.

You must renew your mind, convince yourself there are better views and better alternatives than you presently hold, if only you would explore other knowledge or beliefs. If you experience difficulty, you will tend to see life as difficult. Likewise, if you've experienced hostility, you will tend to see life as hostile, until you began to convince yourself that life has better to offer, that whatever you had in the past was just a setback, and that if you give it a chance, you will begin to experience better life. Perhaps your life has been so difficult. Resolve to change your mind about your difficulty and start to see your better future. Use your mind as your escape route, believing that if you can see it in your mind's eye, you can achieve it.

See that life has better things to offer so, begin to see better potentials from it.

Enough of the suffering mentality. Start to heal. Choose to forgive. Make an effort to keep the past in the past, where it belongs.

Even in going through this exercise, you will feel your burden lift. You will feel lighter and healthier.

Start to see beyond that limitation. Choose to see that there is light at the end of the tunnel, no matter how long the tunnel may be. No matter what, there's always light at the crack of dawn, no matter how dark the night might be. The Bible says, 'Weeping may endure for a night, but joy comes in the morning!' (Psalm 30:5)

So, embrace the joy of the new day. Relish the beauty of the new day. Reach out to the fresh energy of a new day. Let the freshness of a new morning caress you. Yield yourself to the law of the new day. Open up to new opportunities. Don't close your mind. Your change is imminent. Yield to the possibility of a better life. Choose to believe the best. Give life a second chance. You owe yourself a second chance. Forgive. Heal. Draw the curtain on hurt or betrayal or loss or whatever it is that you might have suffered. Step out steadily. Step out graciously. Step out with dignity, even if life has knocked you with indignity. Take your life in your hands. Refuse to be victim the of past hurt or past mistakes. Refuse to be a victim. Come out to new life, to new existence. Believe there's so much potential in you.

Do not delay. There's so much you can give to life, and there's so very much life too can offer you. There's so much you impact. There are so many you can influence. Let your story be another's hope. Be another person's hero. The Bible also says, 'Iron sharpens iron, so shall a friend sharpen the countenance of his friend.' (Proverbs 27:17) Be somebody's inspiration!

Always know that there's someone out there who your truth can also set free, who your victory can encourage. Let your mind believe. Do not hold back.

Your past experience, whatever it may be, should be a springboard to better life, to a better existence. Let your past not be the coffin that buries you. Let it be the ladder that lets you climb higher, to a better life.

Drum it into your belief system: *I'm coming out stronger and better.* Be beautiful again. Be creative again. Be happy again.

Dare to dream again. Snatch your chance from life. Create your own rhythm. Initiate your own dance. Be encouraged. Be unstoppable.

Be your own champion. Be your own hero. Rescue yourself from the doldrums of the past. Let transformation take its course. Allow the whole process. Do not be afraid to laugh again, to love again, to try again. Tell yourself, 'I can do all things.' Rise up. Get up. It's a new life. It's a new hope. It's a new day. It's a transformed you!

Have a change of mind. Break barriers. Have fun. You have greatness deposited in you.

NOTES TO SELF

1. **Everything starts from the mind—ideas, belief, norms, decisions, culture, and so on.**

2. **It is often said, 'You can't do things the same way and expect different results.'**

3. **It will therefore not be an error to say that anyone who does not become transformed or allow themselves the privilege of transformation is 'so yesterday'.**

4. **Transformation is also creating something out of nothing. Ideas (visions) touched with action and resulting in the envisioned reality have encountered the power of transformation!**

5. **When we allow ourselves to be enrolled in the school of transformation, we will be free from the prison of rigidity, of our outdated mentality.**

6. **Break the barriers. Discover new frontiers. Set new targets. Accomplish new goals.**

11. Be Distinguished! Be Different!

If the majority are doing the bare minimum, go the extra mile, be the extra factor. These are the ingredients of excellence. Dare to be positively different. To be distinguished takes a lot of courage and determination. Be determined to be positively different.

I remember when my church back home in Africa was planning to hold a program. The children's church was allotted some time to perform. The children's teacher gave them songs to learn, and the best child would, of course, lead the song. When my daughter showed me the lyrics for the song, I told her to understand what the message in the song was portraying. Secondly, she should learn how to sing the song properly, and finally she would take to the stage and perform the song.

I taught her how to sing the song, how to use her facial expressions, and to know at what point in the song to use hand gestures to deliver the message in the best way possible. At the end of it all, not only was she chosen to lead the song, but she was a blessing to the church at large. Of course, yours truly was made a proud mum.

This scenario implies that whatever one does in life, one should do it extremely well. Develop the mindset of *doing it right the first time and doing it extremely well too*, because there might not be a second chance!

As I said earlier, be the extra factor. If others are wearing plain white, go the extra mile of bleaching, starching, and pressing your own white to be distinct. Likewise, if everyone is wearing black, make your own extra special by choosing a size that compliments your physique. Make the extra effort to make your presentation a little special. If others are offering a handshake, take yours higher with a kind smile!

Do something in a special way. Make the ordinary special. Make the mundane exhilarating. *Make effort look effortless.* As the saying goes, 'If life gives you lemons, make lemonade.' If it tosses you an orange, make an orange slush!

If others are carefree, decide to be careful. If others are late-comers, choose to be an early bird. Raise the bar for yourself. Be smart. Be savvy. Be honest. Be determined. Add self-respect and dignity. Then you're truly distinguished!

It is good to set oneself apart for good things. As I said earlier, 'Turn the ordinary into the extraordinary.'

The decision to be distinguished must not stem from a mindset of arrogance or superiority. Rather, it should stem from a simple, humble heart that aspires to achieve something better in life.

It takes hard work and conscientiousness to be distinguished. Your stance might not necessarily make you popular or appreciated, especially if you're surrounded by mediocre or 'average minded' people. Just remind yourself that you're not doing it for 'them'; rather, you're cultivating a new culture for 'you', which will serve as a vehicle to transport you to your goal.

Understand that mediocrity is never found at the top, and you will easily identify the type of crowd that surrounds you. Determine not to be distracted from reaching the top. Only the distinguished few have places at the top, and they are unfortunately few in comparison to the world population. Choose to be among them.

In your bid to be different, opposition may arise. Stand your ground. Know what you believe. Remember, you have a destination.

Stay focused, because if you pause to think and assess things from the proper perspective, you will realize that the opposition often stems from a mindset of mediocrity, envious people who surreptitiously desire to be just like you but lack the courage. These people lack the courage to venture into the mode you've set for yourself.

Your being different should be positive, deliberate, and strategic. Be conspicuous. No one operates in obscurity to stand out. As the Scriptures say, 'You can't hide a lamp under a heap' (Matt. 5:15).

Map out how you want to achieve your goal. Acquire more skills if necessary, more research, more education, more knowledge. Add more creativity, more enthusiasm, more charm, more personality, more positivity.

In honesty, be transparent.
In relationship, be sincere.
In modesty, be appealing.
In principle, be astute.

Create an aura around you that is authentic, that cannot be compromised nor replicated. Be excitingly different, refreshing and appealing. This is a mark that will positively set you apart. Be determined to be honest while others are being crooked. Exhibit excellence amid mediocrity. Be the reference point of knowledge while others are clueless.

Be outstanding. Only the outstanding are exemplary. Only the outstanding are worthy of emulation.

Don't be normal. Normal people follow the norm. Be exceptional. Exceptional people do ordinary things in extraordinary ways.

Be the solution the universe is desperate for!

NOTES TO SELF

1. To be distinguished takes a lot of courage and determination. Be determined to be positively different.
2. Develop the mindset of doing it right the first time and doing it extremely well too, because there might not be a second chance!
3. Do something in a special way. Make the ordinary special. Make the mundane exhilarating. Make effort look effortless.
4. If life gives you lemons, make lemonade.' If it tosses you an orange, make an orange slush!
5. Raise the bar for yourself.
6. In honesty, be transparent. In relationship, be sincere. In modesty, be appealing. In principle, be astute.
7. Be outstanding. Only the outstanding are exemplary. Only the outstanding are worthy of emulation.
8. Be the solution the universe is desperate for.

12. Your Attitude Equals Your Altitude!

Dictionary.com defines attitude as 'manner, disposition, feeling, position, and so on, with regard to a person or thing.'

Attitude is your disposition to a situation or event (tragic or otherwise) it is how you decide to behave or handle any given situation after your initial natural reaction.

So, we can safely say attitude is not inherent but developed.

Life is unpredictable, with its many curves, but we should be predictable in the way we handle life's surprises.

It's important to determine that 'come what may', whatever curveball life chooses to throw at me, I will remain positive, hopeful. No matter how bad the situation is, I choose to see the light at the end of the tunnel.

I like the Hindi attitude of *sab theek ho jaayega*, meaning 'it will be alright', should definitely be one's attitude. If life decides to visit with its unpleasantness, remain positive and refuse to give in to distress.

It is important to note, it is natural and human to express sadness when something untoward happens. It is good to shed tears if they bring relief, but what we should not permit is the feeling of despair. The Holy Scriptures perfectly spell out the attitude we should adopt in the face of adversity:

> *We are pressed hard on every side; but not crushed, perplexed; but not in despair, persecuted; but not abandoned, struck down; but not destroyed.* (2 Corinthians 4:8–9 NIV)

Despair robs one of hope and the joy of seeing the positive side of a situation. It may sound difficult, but from my perspective, given my experience, I know it's not hard.

Nevertheless, how you control a situation that comes your way says a lot about you. How you choose to comport yourself matters a lot, and the positive vibes you're able to garner to yourself in such situation will determine how soon you're ready to come out of it.

Positivity has a huge role to play if you plan to attain great heights in life. Positive mindset, positive attitude, positive energy, positive vibes—the list is endless. Surround yourself with everything positive, until you begin to see mountains (challenges, problems, difficulties) as stepping stones to better things.

How you choose to see, and handle a given situation largely determines the ultimate outcome. How we respond to things says a lot about who we are. Will we choose to be constructive and positive about how we handle anything that comes our way, or will we choose to be negative? Will we choose to be in control of our emotions as things unravel around us, or will we give in to rage and sorrow?

How we manage our circumstances, or our 'hurt', and choose to see the positive side of things—as the game player would say, 'keep your head in the game'—is vital for our well-being. By choosing to keep your head in the game, by being calm and not reactive or impulsive, you will accomplish a lot.

Choose to be cool and calm when attending to issues. Adopt the 'whatever comes in my way in life, I choose to see things in a positive perspective' attitude (especially when it comes to things, I don't have power over or full details about). I choose to let myself be in control and not vice versa. No matter what comes my way, either positive or otherwise, I choose to be the master of my game instead of my game 'mastering me', being on top of my situation all the time.

This stance has helped me, and continues to help me, through life challenges. No matter how bad the situation may be, no matter what difficulties I come across, it's my choice not to despair.

It helps a lot. We expend lesser energy being on top of a situation instead of the other way around. We tend to be under immense pressure, feeling suffocated.

It seems there's no solution in sight when we allow a situation to get the better of us. No matter the surprises life throws at us, choose not to be the victim. Work a way out. 'Get a better deal' out of a bad situation. Choose not to be rigid or unbending. Refuse to be unforgiving or be the victim. Instead, choose to look for a solution.

It is essential to have the right attitude in life. Our attitude actually acts as a propeller in our life's journey. If we develop the correct disposition towards things, even when no solution is in sight, we'll be amazed that our positive stance always attracts the right energy/ solution. Refuse to wear the burden of life's issues. Don't allow yourself to be pressured to the point of hopelessness.

We should not allow what we go through to weigh us down. Choose the right attitude towards things. Then life becomes more bearable and agreeable.

Your attitude determines where you go and how far you can get in life. If you choose to be vengeful, hateful, hurtful, or negative, everything will be bleak and black, and because of this, you might not attract the support you require. After all, nobody wants to be around a negative person. Nobody is attracted to negativity.

So, put aside bitterness, offence, excessive guilt, self-pity, self-condemnation, or whatever negative feelings you may be tempted to entertain. This does not mean denying your situation; you must take ownership of whatever situation you find yourself. However, you must choose a better tool to handle a discouraging situation. This is vital to how far you can go and how quickly you can get out of that unsavoury situation. So, consciously work on yourself.

Choose to have the right attitude. The right attitude is attractive to many people and attracts more positivity.

Choose to work on your hurt. Choose to work on your guilt. Choose to work or receive help concerning that trauma. You don't want to live in negativity. Choose to work on your heart so that it does not degenerate to bitterness or unforgiveness. Choosing not to make excuses for the cause of your misfortune is being the bigger person.

Nobody wants to be around someone who's always sad, always angry, exuding negative vibes all the time. Decide that, no matter how bad the situation may get, you will choose to be on top of it, you will not be a victim. With that kind of attitude, it is likely that the desired help will come. The positive disposition will attract a positive response. It's important to attract every ounce of positivity you can.

There are a million and one reasons why everything negative should seen as negative and therefore handled with negativity. However, if you choose to approach such a situation differently, you will be amazed at how quickly you heal and how quickly you overcome.

If you choose to be the bigger person, to forgive an offence, to forgo any form of animosity towards the person or entity that caused you loss, if you so choose to rise above setbacks and see yourself as a victor rather than the victim, not to adopt the principle of 'an eye for an eye', if you choose reconciliation in the place of revenge, choose empathy in place of offence, choose sensibility in the place of selfishness, choose love in the place of hate, choose resilience in the place of complaints, choose encouragement in the place of discouragement, choose light instead of darkness, choose God in place of the devil, choose optimism in place of misery, choose to be noble rather than egoistic, choose sensitivity over brashness, choose a constructive attitude over angry outburst, you will be amazed at how the entire scenario will change for the better!

Your attitude will invariably determine how high your achievement will be. Let your attitude guide you to your desired height. Let your attitude be your strength rather than your weakness. Let it be the propeller that lifts you to a greater destiny.

Your attitude is your choice!

NOTES TO SELF

1. Attitude is not inherent but developed.
2. Life is unpredictable, with its many curves, but we should be predictable in the way we handle life's surprises.
3. Nevertheless, how you control a situation that comes your way says a lot about you.
4. Positivity has a huge role to play if you plan to attain great heights in life. Positive mindset, positive attitude, positive energy, positive vibes
5. if you choose to approach such a situation differently, you will be amazed at how quickly you heal and how quickly you overcome.
6. choose to be the bigger person, to forgive an offence, to forgo any form of animosity towards the person or entity that caused you loss.
7. Your attitude is your choice!

13. Let Hope Have a Place! (This Too Shall Pass)

Sometimes life is full of crisis and there *seems* to be no way out. It looks as if life is filled with predicaments and there's no end in sight. Everywhere one looks, there's discouragement. The news is full of not so good news—hate and war crimes, and so on. Note that I used the word *seems*, because in my life's journey, I have realized that the one who created us did not create us without hope. However, the weight of the pressure we are facing beclouds our vision so that we cannot see the way out.

There was a story of a man around 1000 BC which was a great inspiration for me in my struggling days. (It still is an inspiration.) He had been anointed to be king. In that era, the choice of a new king was signified by pouring of specially processed olive oil, called the anointing oil, on his head. This signifies that such anointed person is the 'chosen one' or next in line to the throne.

This man's name was David. Even though he was the

'chosen one', he faced many adversities before he could eventually get to the throne. On the one hand was the incumbent king who despised him for no legitimate reason and was after his life at all cost. Because of this, David had to leave the city to become a fugitive in the wilderness. On the other hand, there were civil wars all about him, even in the back of beyond where he is taking refuge. **That is in spite of hiding out of the reach of his pursuers, conflicts never left him.**

One fine day, when he had just won a war and was heading back to his hideout in the wilderness, he discovered his abode had been raided and his family, and that of the band of men that were with him, were being held hostage. On realizing this unsavoury development, his friends became incensed against him and threatened to mob him. What could be worse than this?

Anyone in such a situation might not only be hopeless but severely depressed. Instead, history had it that despite all the troubles around him, David encouraged himself in the Lord! (1 Samuel 30:6 KJV) He gave place to hope.

In our modern time, perhaps the trouble is not physical war or prisoners of war. Perhaps it is the trouble of joblessness, indebtedness, ill health, family troubles, relationship woes, career challenges, substance abuse, financial crisis—the list is endless. Often these troubles don't come singly. They come in multiples.

Whatever the case may be, remind yourself of that one time when you probably had it together, when you had great aspirations for your future and thought you would achieve this or that dream; draw strength from that one time and build up hope from there. Use that as a source of encouragement.

You must look within and revisit the dream, bring it up and dare to dream again even though you don't look like your dream right now, even though it appears unattainable. Bring that dream up again and draw hope from it. Dare to dream again. Dare to hope again. Dare the improbable. Dare the impossible!

Let your past dream give you hope. Let other people's truths inspire you. Draw strength from like minds. Draw inspiration from others who fought and conquered. Tell yourself, 'If they could do it, so can I.'

Keep conquering the little enemies before taking on the big ones. Take a step each day toward achieving your feat, and on each landing, be your own cheerleader.

Nothing in life lasts forever. Nothing continues forever. At some point, a change surfaces. No matter the hardship, suffering, or challenge, even the present world has a terminal date!

No matter how long a journey is, there's a terminal point. Nothing in life, as the saying goes, is permanent. Even certain activities or indulgences that gave one pleasure at some point become boring or uninteresting. As the saying goes, 'No condition is permanent.' Be encouraged that whatever setback or you are facing will not last forever. It has a terminal date!

Likewise, whatever is giving me displeasure now will not last forever. Most often, the terminal date of a situation will be solely dependent on the actions one takes. Whatever life situation we find ourselves, we can decide: the time for that negative experience is up *now*!

You might be asking, 'How?' Assess and reassess the situation in which you find yourself. Ask yourself these questions:

- How did I get here?
- How can I make things better?
- Am I in a place where I am not valued?
- Can this be the reason for my de-motivation?
- Am I currently in a disrespectful friendship, abusive relationship, family, or place of employment?
- Have I allowed things to become toxic in a bid to 'endure' or be 'longsuffering'?

Now, tell yourself:

I have a choice to get out of such toxic situation. I am the main actor in this scene. I can determine when to 'halt' or 'cut' in order to step out of unhealthy situation. I am the driver of my life. Nobody else will determine the direction my life is going. I can decide to halt, pause, or quit totally. So, I choose to pull out of every negativity.

Yes, there's a place for longsuffering. There's a place for endurance. But there's also a point of decision-making, the point at which we say, 'Enough is enough!'

When we start to see life's challenges in this light, we can begin to move on, to step out of every suffering or unhealthy pattern.

Walk out of every abuse or toxicity. No book in life counsels one to endure abuse to the point of loss of life or limb. Speak up to that bullying boss in a respectful way. Step up to that abusive friend today, in a nonviolent way. Decide the terminal point of all 'undesirables' in your life.

While you are at it, decide: I will not be down forever. This shall not last. I will not be jobless forever. I will not be childless forever. This undesirable situation shall not outlive me. This unwarranted situation shall not last. I will make a rebound.

I may have to start small. I may have to start all over again. I may have to use my talents instead of my huge 'qualifications'. I will get up, dust myself off, and keep running my race until I get to the top. I will not stop until my good becomes better and my better best.

Perhaps it is a loss of a loved one. This can be traumatic to the point of feeling lost. In as much as tragedy is not desirable, we encounter one at some point in life. We owe it to the loved one lost to keep living meaningfully to preserve their memories in a most loving and positive way. Some people set up trusts or perform some form of charity work to preserve their loved one's memories. It is most rewarding to find that such loved ones, even in death, are affecting lives, and our own lives will attain new meaning.

By refusing to be dejected or in despair, we have won over that situation and have not allowed the undesirable situation to outlast us. We have become champions!

No matter the trial, the temptation, the travail, tell yourself, 'This too shall pass.'

Pull yourself out of the doldrums and begin to create a nice, healthy environment for yourself. Take the reins of your life back. Set up a game plan, starting with the most achievable goals. In a short while, when you look back, you'll be amazed the milestones you've achieved!

Refuse to be held back. Get the necessary help. Don't go it alone. Want to drop habitual drinking? Call Alcoholics Anonymous. Feeling suicidal? Call the Samaritans. Drug addiction or other addictions? Go for help now! Are you bereaved? Call a helpline for bereavement. Abused? Call the authorities. Go out and talk to somebody. Don't let that situation send you on a downward spiral. Tell yourself, 'This too shall pass', and pass it shall.

Keep your hope alive.

NOTES TO SELF

1. Whatever the case may be, remind yourself of that one time when you probably had it together.
2. Bring that dream up again and draw hope from it. Dare to dream again. Dare to hope again. Dare the improbable. Dare the impossible!
3. I have a choice to get out of such toxic situation. I am the main actor in this scene. I can determine when to 'halt' or 'cut' in order to step out of unhealthy situation.
4. I may have to start small. I may have to start all over again.
5. No matter the trial, the temptation, the travail, tell yourself, 'This too shall pass.'
6. Keep your hope alive.

14. Don't Conform!

Don't conform to others' expectations of you when they are not in consonance with your expectations of yourself. Being politically correct (in this context) originates from not being true to oneself. It stems from being 'part of the crowd' and failing to distinguish yourself.

You don't have to be politically correct. That is what the world expects! *Don't do this. Don't do that. Don't talk this way. Don't think that way. This is not acceptable.*

Many of us have been deprived of our freedom to be real or true ourselves because of man-made expectations that do not possess any human value. *This does not conform to societal norms or that does not meet societal expectations.* Don't let anyone force you into protocols you have no business with.

The expectation of the one that created you is that you are uniquely correct. If it makes you feel better, always remember that the world population is about 7 billion. Not one of these in the populace is the same as you.

Identify your path and pursue it with dexterity, doggedness, and sincerity.

The same world that expects you to be 'politically correct' is the same that will applaud your success. Don't conform!

Don't lose your positive ideals. Make people respect your ideals.

The world is already confused, and it's just looking for more people to confuse. Don't join the bandwagon of the confused.

Having to conform to others' expectations usually robs you of your individuality and deprives you of the harmony that comes with being you. Nothing can compare to the original. Nothing can compare with being you, so stop conforming to institutional expectation. Instead, be true to yourself and the purpose for which you are created.

My dad expected me to become a qualified and successful accountant. Unfortunately, for the best part of my young adult life, I struggled to be that picture. It wasn't until much later on in life, after many struggles, failures, and disappointments that I finally figured out what I was cut out to be.

Some years back, I watched Beyoncé's life documentary on television. I learned how her mum and dad discovered her talent quite young and encouraged her from a tender age to pursue her passion in the world of entertainment. My serious thought as I was watching the program was, 'What would have become of Beyoncé if her parents had forced her to be a doctor or a nurse?' The world would have been deprived of one of the most talented entertainers ever to live!

Imagine Cristiano Ronaldo dos Santos Aveiro's parents encouraging him to become a teacher. The world would have been deprived of one of the best talents in the field of football.

When you conform to what you're not, you rob the world of an original!

Conforming to the world's ideal is like wearing an oversized garment or oversized shoes—it just doesn't fit.

Search for yourself and find yourself. Fear and lack of self-confidence are some of the major hindrances to reinventing oneself. Another is the false notion of age. No one is too old or too young to reinvent oneself. Find your purpose and stay true to yourself. Stand out (positively), stand tall, and be you.

Give the world a full dose of you, what the unique you are made of.

NOTES TO SELF

1. Being politically correct (in this context) originates from not being true to oneself.
2. The expectation of the one that created you is that you are uniquely correct.
3. Don't let anyone force you into protocols you have no business with.
4. Identify your path and pursue it with dexterity, doggedness, and sincerity.
5. The world is already confused, and it's just looking for more people to confuse.
6. When you conform to what you're not, you rob the world of an original!
7. Conforming to the world's ideal is like wearing an oversized garment or oversized shoes—it just doesn't fit.

15. Reposition Yourself

No matter what the setback is, there's always a rebound. There's always a point of coming back. It's very important that after certain setbacks in life, there's a need to reposition oneself. This is a key to moving ahead. Look back to see where things went wrong, and with the eyes of faith, look ahead to where you want to be. And then, right here in the middle of the past and the future— this place called the present—reposition yourself to get to that beautiful future. You're not helpless or clueless anymore. You have a potent weapon at hand right now, in the present, called the power of hindsight. You stand in the position of correcting past mistakes. If we don't reposition ourselves, there's no way we can correct the errors of the past to move ahead into that great future we have envisioned for ourselves.

It's imperative for anyone craving to move ahead in life to be repositioned. This is because our former positioning was not at a vantage point in the first instance. That was why things didn't work out! Stepping out of the past, standing in the present to take positive steps into the future, not doing things the way we did them in the past. There is a saying: 'You cannot keep doing something same way and expect a different result.'

Having the right attitude and being in the right mindset will help you to project powerfully into the future. When a basketball player wants to shoot the ball into the basket, he positions himself to shoot the ball above the rim so that it falls into it. Likewise, a footballer who wants to score into the net will position himself to shoot the ball into the net, just as an athlete in the high jump positions himself to run a distance, then charges forward to propel his whole body up to take that winning leap. Anyone that wants to succeed in life will most certainly reposition themselves from the point where it was not working to achieve their future goal or purpose.

When you see a certain way or style is not working, it's imperative to assess the situation and get in the right position to do it better.

We cannot stay in the same place and think things will work themselves out. Repositioning is akin to changing the method of what was not working.

It's time, like the Phoenix rising from the ashes of the past. Rise from the past heartbreak, defeats, mistakes, meltdowns, or whatever difficulties you faced. Right now, what's important is self-forgiveness and self-acceptance. Rise from the ashes of the past and choose to soar like an eagle. Make a promise to yourself: 'I will be better.'

The Phoenix is a mythical bird. It is believed to live for decades before it bursts into flame. This bird is believed to possess the strange ability to rebirth itself from its burnt ashes. This is a picture of hope, whose message is loud and clear: no matter how bad a situation is, or no matter how 'dead' a situation is, there's still hope of revival (and *survival*). So, put on your new 'skin' and leave the ashes of the past behind. Leave well enough alone and move on. Set new targets, have a new focus, gain new hope, develop new faith, attain new heights.

Pep yourself, believe again, make a commitment to do it better this time around.

It is very important to consciously uncouple oneself from the setbacks of the past, purposely forgiving all parties involved (system, friends, family, self?). As someone rightly said, 'When other people begin to count your mistakes, they should look back and start from their own side, which could be so long that, at the end of the day, they won't have enough time to recount those of others.'

Having said that, we must also learn from past mistakes and take the lessons learnt on board.

When the Phoenix rebirths itself, it 'flies away' from the ashes of its past and forges a new identity, never wallowing in self-pity or reminiscing over its past life. We must adopt the Phoenix code and forge ahead, forming new alliances where necessary, networking, linking with people of like mind, setting new goals, working out strategies for delivering these new goals, identifying need for new skill acquisition or new knowledge.

It is important to let go of the past completely because starting afresh could literarily mean starting over. This might mean going back to the very beginning or starting small. This can be very uncomfortable, because 'ego' or self-pity may want to rear its ugly head. It is good to spur oneself on, turning a blind eye to that negative feeling or thought process.

I always wanted to study law in my secondary school days. It was very unfortunate that was not to be. It wasn't that I did not do well as a student; however, I could not get the support I needed to actualize this dream. When I eventually could, the thought of starting over became my undoing. I reasoned that 'my mates' had graduated and had a career while I was contemplating starting over.

What I had failed to realize then was that my mates would not run my race for me. Neither would I theirs.

Fear and lack of self-confidence (boldness) are major hindrances to reinventing oneself. Another is the excuse of age. No one is too old to reinvent oneself. Never be too old for change.

It doesn't matter if others have run a thousand mile ahead of you. What matters is that you make the effort and take the necessary action to reach your own finish line. If it is important to go back to the beginning of the race, do turn back and begin again. Who says you can't overtake the 'overtakers' (i.e., the ones that have achieved that task before you)?

Accept past mistakes, work on it—or contrary to it, if need be—to achieve a totally different (positive) result, using past mistakes as stepping stones to greater heights.

Sometimes you have to pursue life for it to deliver you what you desire or deserve. Repositioning yourself means being strategic, deliberate, calculated, and focused on your goal without wavering or compromise.

You must put yourself in line of your aspirations. Desires are not often fulfilled when you are sitting at home with the blues. Whatever you desire in life, work smart and work hard for it.

Create and recreate opportunities for yourself. Sometimes the desired target does not come easy.

NOTES TO SELF

1. No matter what the setback is, there's always a rebound.
2. Look back to see where things went wrong, and with the eyes of faith, look ahead to where you want to be.
3. a footballer who wants to score into the net will position himself to shoot the ball into the net.
4. It's time, like the Phoenix rising from the ashes of the past.
5. It doesn't matter if others have run a thousand mile ahead of you. What matters is that you make the effort and take the necessary action to reach your own finish line.
6. Sometimes you have to pursue life for it to deliver you what you desire or deserve.

16. Burn the Bridge

To forge ahead, you must conclude in your mind that you will *burn the bridge.*

Burn the bridge between the past and the present so that it does not have an adverse effect on the future. It is aptly said, 'Drastic times calls for drastic measures' This is why we must consciously sever ties with unpleasant experience or trauma and forcefully forge ahead. Consciously and deliberately burn the bridge that tie you to a negative past, filled with errors, hurts, abuse, fear, and so on. Burn the bridge between the old fearful, helpless, 'incompetent' you and the new powerful, determined, and courageous you. Let the old you rest in peace (and in pieces) so you will not be tempted to piece it together or run back to your comfort zone.

Start over again. There's this saying by the elders in my home country which is so very apt: *Ba o ku, ise o tan,* meaning 'If we still have breath, we can achieve more.' In other words, 'Where there's life, there's hope.' Take a step of faith, and the rest, as they say, will become history!

Forget the loss, forget the cost; otherwise, you won't move forward. Reconnect with yourself, find yourself, and be reconciled with yourself.

Dream again and start putting bits together that will enable you achieve it. The actualization of a dream starts with a step. Show me your faith, and I'll how you my faith by my works (James 2:18).

Determine that the burnt bridge will be the stepping stone you need. Let it be the starting point to the new you could achieve. Let it be the catapult that will fling you up to higher things and achieving greater feats in life. Don't underestimate your own abilities in the midst of so much criticism or judgement. It is amazing that the things you let get into you or define you don't have your strength of character or resilience. Neither do they have your stamina.

Therefore, is it not making a joke of your own capabilities to allow the 'lesser' to determine the fate of the 'greater'?

Do yourself a favour and delete from your mind all the negativity you stored there and begin to chart your own course. Whatever you do, do it for you—and you alone. *Forge ahead and never ever look back!*

NOTES TO SELF

1. Burn the bridge between the past and the present so that it does not have an adverse effect on the future.
2. Consciously and deliberately burn the bridge that tie you to a negative past, filled with errors, hurts, abuse, fear,
3. Burn the bridge between the old fearful, helpless, 'incompetent' you and the new powerful, determined, and courageous you.
4. Determine that the burnt bridge will be the stepping stone you need.
5. It is amazing that the things you let get into you or define you don't have your strength of character or resilience. Neither do they have your stamina.

17. Turn Your Idea into Your Reality

There could be something eating you up right now—some fantasy, some idea, some dream you had way back, some thought you've been playing with that is gradually forming into something bigger in your mind, something you've been wanting to do. So, turn your ideas into your reality. Loads of people went to higher formal educational institutions (university, college, and so on) at the behest of their parents or guardians, teachers or career advisers. They went on to study the 'advised' course yet they feel something is lacking. That thing that is lacking should be pursued, because you might just find out that is where your fulfilment lies.

It has been shown that many people don't really know what they eventually want to do until adulthood; only a few lucky ones get it right from inception. So whatever idea you've been nurturing could just be the next big thing.

Maybe you've got some idea going on in your mind.

Why not explore it and give it expression? You might make something big out of this, or you could improve on that thought, comment, or idea. Maybe it's time you sat down and began to strategize, to see the bigger picture and turn that into the next big thing.

It has often been said that every creative phenomenon started as an idea. Breathe on your idea, birth it. That idea could be a means of livelihood for a thousand people. Perhaps that idea is the antidote needed for someone's meaningful existence. It could be the answer to many people's dilemma.

Turn that idea into your reality.

I've personally had thoughts which God had helped me with and which have become my pleasant realities today. Some don't believe God talks, so maybe that beautiful idea toying at the back of your head is your God-given solution to the world. It's high time we began to look inwards and see the real stuff we are made of. Many people have said their inventions were 'an accident' that later on became a miracle—a global phenomenon.

Recently, I was listening to this young lady, Yemi Alade, on Yanga TV. That was my first time of matching her name to her face. She said she went to Enugu, in the eastern part of Nigeria, to record her single, 'Johnny'. Before she got back to Lagos, the song was leaked. She said she did not know the intention of the person that leaked the song, but that same leaked song launched her into the international music scene.

So, who knows? That 'silly' idea you're toying with

could be the next big thing. Why not get to work and see where it leads to?

You'll be amazed what impact your idea can have in this beautiful planet we call our world.

Don't let your ideas or your talents go to the grave with you. Don't be afraid. At most, if it's not worth investing in, you will at least have no regrets in the future. Explore your options so that there are no future regrets.

There is so much potential to be harnessed. Lots of ground to break through, so many barriers to burst. Don't bottle that idea. See what can be birthed from it. Much greatness has come from little ideas. It could be the catalyst that will take our world to the next level. It will only be what it's meant to be when it is expressed. Don't bottle that idea. Don't be afraid. Explore it to the last.

Take self-doubt and fear out of the equation. Take the thought, *This could fail,* out of the equation. What if it doesn't fail? If other great inventors had given in to their fears, perhaps tools that now affect the globe, like Facebook, Microsoft, various e-platforms, smart gadgets, and so on, would not have been in born into existence.

You have to take a leap of faith. For you to achieve your goal, you must first make the effort of taking the initial step. Things like self-doubt cannot keep getting in the way. You need determination to do away with the status quo!

Obey your guts. Follow your instinct and dare to live your reality. Dare to make your idea your reality.

NOTES TO SELF

1. Maybe you've got some idea going on in your mind. Why not explore it and give it expression? You might make something big out of this

2. It has often been said that every creative phenomenon started as an idea.

3. Don't let your ideas or your talents go to the grave with you. Don't be afraid. At most, if it's not worth investing in, you will at least have no regrets in the future. Explore your options so that there are no future regrets.

4. You have to take a leap of faith. For you to achieve your goal, you must first make the effort of taking the initial step. Things like self-doubt cannot keep getting in the way.

5. Obey your guts. Follow your instinct and dare to live your reality. Dare to make your idea your reality.

Epilogue: Dust Yourself Off— The Show Is About to Start

Such confidence, such assurance!

I didn't gain this in one day. I wish I knew twenty years ago what I know today. I would have spared myself some pain and regrets. However, the favour I eventually did myself was to determine within myself that the reign of terror was over. I made a choice not to be abused, intellectually, emotionally, or psychologically. I chose courage over fear. I recognized I needed help and submitted myself to the support available to me. I chose healing over hurt, forgiveness over offence, and wisdom over foolishness. As I discovered, we all need mentors in life, and it's better late than never.

Winners don't have negative attitude. They don't allow the negativity of their situation to hold them down.

They bounce back. They come back stronger, better, and more determined. It is easier to allow self-pity to gain its ground and begin to wallow in it. Truly, it is not the end of life. I'd say it is the beginning of it!

Gather your courage, your new resolve to start afresh, with your newfound confidence to move on in life. Take the lessons of the past failures and (successes); the time has come to put all these ingredients together and have the show of your life.

Trying again and again is the first and last step to success!

It's time to find purpose. It's time to find fulfilment.

So, get up!

Stay focused, acquire fresh energy, and let the show begin.

Go—to fulfil goals set.

Go—to fulfil lifelong dreams and aspirations.

Go—to fulfil every whim of yours.

Go—to fulfil those 'silly dreams' you feel you can no longer achieve.

Put on your 'helmet of adventure'. Let the adrenalin begin to pump.

Go and be an accomplishment. Remember, accomplishment is not conquering the whole world. Accomplishment is conquering your own fears and insecurities, your inhibitions and limitations.

Remember, if your potential is captain of fifty, go forth and captain your fifties; and if a thousand, captain your thousands.

It's time to be a trail blazer. It's time to break norms and start a new trend, propound a new theory.

Throw the shades back on life. Prove a point to yourself that you are an overcomer, a winner, a champion!

Go and be the next success story. And please share your story with me.

God bless you!
Adekemi Giwa

www.ingramcontent.com/pod-product-compliance
Lightning Source LLC
Chambersburg PA
CBHW031130250726
48655CB00002B/598